PRESENTED TO:

_____

BY:

_____

ON:

_____

CELEBRATING THE NAME ABOVE ALL NAMES

O COME A LET US ADORE HIM

Melody Carlson

ILLUSTRATIONS BY Tony Meers

CROSSWAY BOOKS · WHEATON, ILLINOIS
A DIVISION OF GOOD NEWS PUBLISHERS

O Come Let Us Adore Him

Text copyright © 2000 by Melody Carlson

Illustration copyright © 2000 by Tony Meers

Published by Crossway Books
A division of Good News Publishers
1300 Crescent Street
Wheaton, Illinois

Design: Cindy Kiple

First printing, 2000

Printed in the United States of America

ISBN 1-58134-200-4

Bible quotations indicated as from NASB are taken from the *New American Standard Bible*, © 1960, 1962, 1963, 1968, 1971, 1972, 1973, 1975 and 1977 by The Lockman Foundation.
Bible quotations indicated as from NCV are taken from the *New Century Version*, © 1987, 1988, 1991 by Word Publishing.

Bible quotations indicated as from NIV are taken from the *New International Version*®. Copyright © 1973, 1978, 1984 by International Bible Society. Used by permission of Zondervan Publishing House. All rights reserved. The "NIV" and "New International Version" trademarks are registered in the United States Patent and Trademark Office by International Bible Society. Use of either trademark requires the permission of International Bible Society.

Bible quotations indicated as from NKJV are taken from the *New King James Version*, © 1979, 1980, 1982 by Thomas Nelson.

Bible quotations indicated as from NLT are taken from the *New Living Translation*, © 1996 by Tyndale Charitable Trust.

Bible quotations indicated as from NRSV are taken from the *New Revised Standard Version*, copyright © 1989 by the Division of Christian Education of the National Council of Churches of Christ in the United States of America.

Bible quotations indicated as from TLB are taken from *The Living Bible*, © 1971, 1986 by Tyndale House Publishers.

To Jim and Renée Boeshans

Thanks for all those times

you opened your home to all of us

during the holidays!

TABLE OF CONTENTS

❧ · ❧

FOREWORD

༄ • ༄

The Christmas season is a wonderful time when family and friends gather, share gifts of love, and open their hearts to one another. More than anything else, it should be full of sweet fellowship with our Savior and Lord. But in our fast-paced culture and busy lives, we often crowd Jesus out of the season.

Open the pages of *O Come Let Us Adore Him* and experience original poems, wonderful stories, beautiful illustrations, and reflections on the names of Christ. As you make the person and work of Jesus Christ central to Christmas, the Lord will speak to your family in special ways. By focusing on twelve of the unique names that the Bible applies to Jesus, you will grow to know Him better and love Him more deeply.

As you revisit the wonderful expressions in this book year after year, you will develop enduring family traditions and help your children know Jesus in a strong and personal way.

Barbara Rainey
Co-founder of FamilyLife

For unto us

a Child is born . . . .

And His name

will be called

Wonderful, Counselor,

Mighty God,

Everlasting Father,

Prince of Peace

ISAIAH 9:6 (NKJV)

INTRODUCTION

Even before the beginning of time, God knew He would send His Son to be born on earth. God realized that the world He would so lovingly create would desperately need a Savior. For centuries prophets spoke in mysterious metaphors or word pictures, foretelling again and again the One to come. They called this One by a multitude of names, as if His very being were too great, too magnificent, to be contained in one single, limited word or phrase. And the words they used for His name were symbolic of the character qualities and gifts that He would manifest to a hungry and needy world. He was referred to as the Bread of Life, the Rock of Salvation, the Good Shepherd—and in many, many other ways. These descriptive names became beautiful, living word pictures, showing us who Jesus Christ really is and what His nature is truly like.

The purpose of this book is to remind you and your family of who Jesus is. Christmas can become an overly busy time when we find ourselves asking, "What's the true meaning of Christmas?" My hope is that by taking time to understand and celebrate the many names of Jesus in the form of poetry, text, and art, your family's perspective on Christmas will be eternally enriched—and that your hearts will be changed forever.

Blessings!

Melody Carlson

Who is this child? Who can He be?

He sleeps in a manger carved from a tree.

Can it be true that He came from afar?

And why is the night sky lit by a star?

Who is this one, from heaven above?

Sent down from the Father to show us His love?

Who is this child? His name, can you tell?

His name shall be called Immanuel.

IMMANUEL

It is the Lord who goes before you;

he will be with you, he will not fail you or

forsake you, do not fear or be dismayed.

DEUTERONOMY 31:8 (RSV)

I Have My Eye On You

'm scared, Papa," said Sara as she hurried to keep up with her father's long steps. With large eyes, she looked toward the big, walled city that kept getting closer and closer. It loomed ahead of her like an enormous stone monster just waiting to swallow her up!

"But we're almost to Jerusalem," said Papa. "Why are you so frightened?"

"What if I get lost again, Papa? Don't you remember the last time I went to the market with Benjamin? He left me all by myself, and I got lost, and I wandered for hours not knowing where he was! I was so frightened. I was afraid I'd never see you and Mama again—ever!"

Papa patted her head. "Don't you worry, little one. Your brother was careless that day. But you know that your papa won't be careless. I am right here with you, and you can be sure I have my eye on you."

Sara watched as Papa's dark eyes looked up and gazed off toward the city gates that were getting closer with each step. *Does he really have his eye on me?* she thought to herself. Just to make absolutely sure, she lingered back a few steps, then ducked down and streaked across the road, quickly hiding herself behind the thick trunk of a nearby olive tree. But within seconds she felt a gentle tap on her shoulder and looked up to see Papa standing over her.

"You found me!" she cried happily.

He laughed. "Yes. I told you I've got my eye on you. And I'm right here. But you need to stick close to me, especially because now there are more travelers around us, and we're getting closer to the city. No more hiding like that, Sara."

"I won't, Papa," she promised as she grabbed his big hand. "I just wanted to be perfectly sure you wouldn't lose me like Benjamin did."

As they approached the city gates, the crowds became thick and noisy, with lots of people and animals all pushing against one another as they entered the big city of Jerusalem. Then just as Papa and Sara entered the gates, a large, hairy goat pressed up against her, knocking her to the ground. But no one seemed to notice as she struggled in the dirt, and the bustling crowd just continued right on past her.

"Papa!" she cried from her spot on the ground as she searched the dozens of dusty sandals for the feet that belonged to her father. "Where are you—"

Just then a strong hand reached down and pulled her up. "I'm right here," he said as he brushed her off. "Are you all right?"

"Yes, and you found me!"

He lifted her up to his shoulders where she could see over the tops of all the people. "You were never lost, Sara," he said. "I was right here the whole time."

Later that day they stopped by the market to buy cheese and fruit for lunch. Papa told Sara to hold onto his sleeve while he paid for their food. But for just an instant she let go as she paused to admire a basket heaped with ruby-red pomegranates. Then she quickly reached back to grab Papa's sleeve. But when she looked up she saw she was holding onto the sleeve of a complete stranger.

"You're not my papa!" she cried with alarm.

The man laughed. "You're right about that."

She let go of the sleeve and looked around in terror, tears quickly gathering in her eyes. "Papa!" she yelled as loudly as she could.

In that same moment she felt a gentle hand upon her head. "I am right here, Sara," said Papa. "But why did you let go of my sleeve like that?"

She looked down at her feet. "I'm sorry, Papa."

They went to sit in the shade beside a big pool of water as they ate their lunch, but Sara was very careful to stay right next to Papa. As she ate her fruit and cheese, she watched the older children laughing and playing around the pool of water. And when she was all finished, she asked her father if she could put her hands into the water.

"Sure," said Papa. "But be very careful. The water is deep even at the edge."

"Don't leave," said Sara.

"You know I'll be right here, just like always," Papa reminded her.

Sara went over and knelt by the pool, dipping her hands into the cool, clear water. She made little slapping splashes, then laughed as the water jumped up and cooled off her toes. Then all of a sudden one of the big boys dashed past and accidentally bumped Sarah.

Splash!

She tumbled right into the pool of water, then went down, down just like a stone. She tried to stand up, but the water was over her head. From beneath the water, she tried to cry out for Papa, but only water filled her mouth. Yet in that same moment she felt a strong pair of arms lifting her up to the surface, up to the air.

She gasped, then cried, "Papa!" as she threw her arms around him. Then she blinked with surprise to see that Papa was also in the pool of water—and like her, he was dripping wet!

She laughed to see rivulets of water pouring down his thick beard. "Papa, you got yourself all wet just to save me!"

He smiled. "Of course, Sara. Did you think I would just sit by and watch you drown?"

She firmly shook her head. "No, Papa. Because I know you are with me, and I know you have your eye on me. And I know you won't let anything bad happen to me—ever!"

So for the rest of the day, Sara never worried one little bit about getting lost or separated from her father. And although she tried to stick close to him, she knew that if she forgot, he would be right there with her. For it was true, he did have his eye upon her! 🕮

IMMANUEL

Many years ago God made a pledge to His children, the Israelites, as they were about to enter their promised land. He told them not to fear anything or anyone in their new homeland because He would always, always be with them, and He would never, ever leave them. But like Sara, it seems that God's children wondered if God really meant what He said or if He could really keep His promise. Time after time they tested their Father in heaven to see if He would keep His word—and God never let them down.

But the children of Israel didn't have the same face-to-face relationship with God that Sara had with her father. God would only call out to them and speak to them through their prophets and leaders. They could only come to Him through sacrifices offered by the priests. But He had made another promise to them—a promise that one day things would be different.

And God kept His word. He sent His Son into the world, and then things changed. When Jesus was born as a tiny, vulnerable baby, God became one of us! He chose to experience what we experience. He plunged into our world out of great love for us. He gave His life so that we might live. And through His life and death, He proved in the most amazing way that He would never leave us or forsake us.

Immanuel means "God with us." But it's not just another name for Jesus. It's our promise that no matter what we may face in life, God will be with us. Always!

Therefore the Lord Himself will give you a sign:
"Behold, the virgin shall conceive and bear a Son,
and shall call His name Immanuel."

ISAIAH 7:14 (NKJV)

OUR PRAYER

Dear God, help us to remember that You are always and forever with us. Sometimes we get lonely or confused, and we forget that You are right here. Please remind us of Your presence with us; and teach us to keep our hearts and minds focused on You. Amen.

Who is this man? What does he say?

"I am the life. I am the way.

Only My truth will set you free.

To come to the Father, you must come through Me."

Who is this man? And what's this about?

He says to go in. He says to go out.

What does it mean? What is it for?

His love is the key. And He is the Door.

THE DOOR

Jesus said to him, "I am the way, the truth, and the life. No one comes to the Father except through Me."

JOHN 14:6 (NKJV)

The Lost Door

⁓ · ⁓

Didn't you have the map?" asked Andrew accusingly.

"I did," said Timothy in a quiet voice.

"Then where is it now?" demanded Andrew.

"I think I lost it."

Andrew looked at the greenery around them, then scowled. "Well, if you lost it, then we must be lost too!"

"I'm sorry," said Timothy. "But I was so tired, it must've slipped from my hand."

The two boys had wandered through the maze of bushes and shrubs and trees in the gigantic walled garden for most of the afternoon. Today was their friend Luke's birthday, and Luke's father had allowed all the kids to explore his enormous garden. "But you must keep your maps with you at all times," he had warned. "And keep track of where you are so you can find your way back to the garden door in time for the party. Don't forget, there is only one door, and this is it." He had stood next to the tall metal door and smiled. "Now, have fun!"

Everyone had eagerly agreed to these rules, and Timothy and Andrew had set out together, with Andrew bragging to all the others about how he planned to explore more of the garden than anyone else. Andrew had led the way, and Timothy felt certain the two boys had walked for miles and miles and miles. Now they were both tired and hungry and thirsty. Only a few minutes ago the sun had dipped down below tree level, and the sky was beginning to grow dusky and purple with evening shadows.

"It's getting dark," said Timothy, trying to hide the fear he felt crawling under his skin.

"I can see that," snapped Andrew. "Unless we find that door, we're going to completely miss Luke's party."

"And we might have to spend the night here," said Timothy with a shudder.

"That looks familiar," said Andrew pointing toward a large clump of ever-green trees. "Let's go that way."

By the time they reached the grove it was nearly dark, and the trees looked like tall, black giants to Timothy. "I don't remember this," he said as a shiver ran down his spine. "And it feels to me like we're going the wrong way."

"Well, which way do you think we should go?"

"That way," Timothy pointed.

"No, this way!" said Andrew. They argued awhile; then both turned and marched off in separate directions.

Timothy walked the way that felt the most familiar to him, but with each step it only grew darker and darker, and soon he could see nothing but dark-ness and shadows. Suddenly he wished he had stayed with Andrew. Even if the other boy was a grump and going the wrong way, being with him would be better than being all alone—and scared. Timothy sat down on a rock and tried not to cry. Instead he looked all around him and listened as carefully as he could, trying to find some clue as to where that big door might be. A few minutes later he was sure he heard something. It sounded almost like music, and he stood and slowly walked toward it, pausing every few steps to be cer-tain of his direction.

After a long time of walking, it seemed like he was no closer than before. He paused once again and strained his ears to listen, but now all he could hear was the lonely whisper of the wind rustling through the trees, the call of a night owl, and the hollow rumbling of his hungry stomach. He did not want to spend the night out here by himself. Oh, why had he been so careless that he lost the map?

Just then he noticed what looked like a glow of lantern light, coming from the same direction where he'd heard music before. So once again he began to walk that way, hoping and praying he was moving toward the door now. But after he'd walked only a short while, he could no longer see any sign of light. And now he wondered if he had just imagined it in the first place.

Finally Timothy just sat down and cried, certain he would never find his way out of here. He wished he'd stayed with the other kids, wished he'd held onto his map. He even wished he'd never gone out with Andrew in the first place. Oh, why had he been so foolish? He wondered if Andrew felt this bad right now, and he hoped that he did, because in many ways this all seemed to be Andrew's fault. After all, he was the one who wanted to keep going when Timothy thought they should head back. And he was the one who insisted that Timothy should carry the map all the time. Well, he hoped Andrew felt as miserable and hungry and scared as he did. It would serve him right!

Just then Timothy heard a noise moving toward him. He'd heard there were lions in these parts, but he'd never seen one. He crouched down low to the ground, wrapping his arms around his head, trembling with fear.

Then suddenly he saw a light through the trees. He stood up to look, and there coming his way was Luke!

"Luke!" cried Timothy, running directly toward his friend. "Am I glad to see you!"

"Where have you been?" asked Luke with concern.

"Lost," said Timothy. "I lost the map. Sorry."

"Well, come with me and I'll take you to the door. You must be starving, and you're missing my party."

So the two boys started out, and Timothy tried not to think about

Andrew. Besides, maybe he'd already found the door. For several steps Timothy said nothing. So what if Andrew was all alone and hungry. But then he knew that was wrong. That's not how he'd want to be treated.

"Did Andrew make it back?" asked Timothy.

"Not when I left the party," said Luke. "Have you seen him?"

"Yeah," said Timothy, stopping in his tracks and turning the other way. "I think he's back there."

The two boys walked a ways, and finally they found Andrew, still sitting in the evergreen grove. He was crying.

"It's us, Andrew," called Luke.

Andrew quickly stood up and wiped the tears from his face. "Thanks for coming back for me," he said, then added, "I'm sorry I wandered so far, Luke. And I'm sorry I was so bossy to you, Timothy."

Timothy smiled, happy that he'd returned to look for his friend. "That's okay."

"So, do you have a map, Luke?" asked Andrew.

Luke laughed. "Oh, I don't need a map. This is my father's garden, and I know my way around here pretty well. I could probably find the door blindfolded."

And in no time Luke led them straight to the door. It hadn't even been that far away. Then the boys both thanked Luke for leaving his birthday party to rescue them.

"Oh, that's okay," said Luke. "My party wasn't much fun with two of my best buddies missing."

"Do you think there's anything left to eat?" asked Timothy hopefully.

"You can count on it," said Luke.

"All right!" exclaimed Andrew. "Let's celebrate!" ❧

THE DOOR

You can probably imagine how afraid Andrew and Timothy must have felt. How frightening it is to be lost in a strange place with no hope of finding your way out. How unnerving to know that friends or family are nearby and yet nowhere to be seen. How terrifying to be all alone with the darkness closing in around you.

But what you may not realize is that apart from Jesus that is what our lives would be like, all the time. The Bible tells us that we are lost, we are without hope, and unless something changes we will be in darkness forever. Just as Andrew and Timothy would have never found their way to the party without Luke, we will never find our way to God without someone's help. And that someone is Jesus.

While here on earth, Jesus came right out and told us that He is "The Door" and "The Way." He is the means of getting from where we are to where we need to go. When we invite Him into our lives, He becomes our way back to God. And that's when we step out of our dark, lonely world and into His wonderful world that is full of warmth and laughter and goodness and light!

But Jesus made it clear that we can only get to the Father by going through Him. He is the only door, and there is no other way to God! Thankfully, He came and now the door to God is open, inviting us all to step through it.

"I assure you, I am the gate for the sheep," he [Jesus] said.

"All others who came before me were thieves and robbers.

But the true sheep did not listen to them.

Yes, I am the gate. Those who come in through me will be saved.

Wherever they go, they will find green pastures."

JOHN 10:7-9 (NLT)

OUR   PRAYER

Dear God, thank You so much for sending Jesus to be the door that takes us directly to You. And we thank You, Jesus, for living inside our hearts. Now we ask that You will always remind us that You are the only way we can ever come to the Father. Amen.

Who is this man who speaks about fruit?
He talks of a vine, the leaves, and the root.
He tells how the branches must cling to the tree.
All this just to show how I should be.

Who is this man? What does He say?
He says to abide. He says to obey.
He says I am His, and that He is mine.
I am the branch, and He is the Vine.

THE TRUE VINE

"I am the true vine, and My Father is the vinedresser.

Every branch in Me that does not bear fruit

He takes away; and every branch that bears fruit

He prunes, that it may bear more fruit. . . ."

JOHN 15:1-2, 4 (NKJV)

The Apple Tree

⁓ ∴ ⁓

Elizabeth's grandmother gave her an apple tree for her first birthday. Now, that might seem a strange gift for a little baby, and the fact is, Elizabeth couldn't even remember getting her tree way back then, although her mother told her she did. But as Elizabeth grew older, she loved her apple tree more and more with each passing year.

Every year when Elizabeth's birthday came, the apple tree would be a little taller and fuller. And when she turned six it bore its first fruit. Three red apples. A small crop, no doubt, but welcome just the same. Elizabeth gently picked the ripe red apples on her birthday, then lovingly carried them into the house and set them in a row on the old table just to admire them off and on during the day.

When supper time came, Elizabeth washed the apples and with her mother's help carefully pared and sliced them to serve to her family. Everyone at the table said "oooh" and "ahh" and "aren't these the best apples you have ever tasted in your entire life!"

The following year Elizabeth's apple tree produced two dozen apples! And on her birthday Elizabeth took out her mother's biggest basket and filled it with all those beautiful red apples. With her mother's help, she used some to bake a birthday pie, some to make a quart of applesauce, and some to pare and slice. And once again everyone thought Elizabeth's apples were the best ever!

At the end of the following winter, Elizabeth's grandfather stopped by her yard and said, "Elizabeth, you really need to prune that little tree of yours."

"Oh, no!" cried Elizabeth in horror. "I could never bear to cut a single twig from my apple tree."

"Well, unhealthy and unfruitful apple branches need to be cut," he explained. "That way good branches can keep bearing lots of apples, and the tree can produce the most fruit possible."

"But that would hurt the tree!" said Elizabeth as she looked at her grandfather's sharp pruning tools.

He scratched his chin thoughtfully, then answered, "Not as much as it will hurt if you don't."

Elizabeth stood in front of her tree. "I just can't let you cut any of the branches. It would be much too painful."

Elizabeth's grandfather shook his head and left. She tried to forget his words. When spring came, her apple tree looked more beautiful than ever, just as white as a cloud, with hundreds of blossoms. Then came summer, and the tree was loaded with dozens and dozens of tiny, green apple buds. By the end of summer all of those apple buds grew into dozens and dozens of rosy little apples. As Elizabeth admired her tree she was sure her grandfather had been wrong.

But as the apples grew bigger and heavier, the tree's overburdened branches began to hang so low that some of them were actually touching the ground. And then a windstorm came along, and the weakened branches began to split and break. Poor Elizabeth ran outside and tried to hold the branches up, attempting to keep them from breaking any more. But finally she knew it was hopeless. And the following morning her little apple tree's branches looked very sad.

By Elizabeth's birthday many of the branches were dead or dying. Rotten apples lay under the tree, and many of the broken and dying branches were now infested with bugs. Elizabeth just sat down next to her tree and sobbed.

"What's the problem?" called out her grandfather.

"My apple tree," sobbed Elizabeth. "Just look at it!"

The one who had warned Elizabeth earlier that year walked up and studied the tree, then made a tsk-tsk sound between his teeth. "Looks pretty bad."

"It's all my fault," she cried. "I should've let you prune it."

"Now you know why some of the branches needed to be removed."

She looked up with pleading eyes. "Can you make it better, Grandfather? Will it ever have any more apples?"

He carefully looked over the tree, inspecting each bough and branch, then finally spoke. "The tree is still as strong as ever, and some of the sturdy branches can be left. But I'll have to remove the ones that have broken away."

She cringed. "But can you do it?"

"Not today. I can't prune when the sap's still flowing."

Grandfather came back after the first frost, and Elizabeth watched as he took out his tools and began to work. Her hand over her mouth, she looked on in horror as he removed limb after limb after limb. Finally she just had to speak. "Can't those limbs be saved?"

"Not when they've pulled clean away from the main tree like that," he answered. "They'll get no sap, no lifeblood, running through them." Then he pointed out some sturdier branches with only small breaks. "But you see these ones?"

She nodded.

"They've managed to hold onto the tree. There's hope for them." He put some gooey liquid on the split spots, then pulled some strips of cloth out of his bag and wound them around the tree, tightening the branches up nice and snug. When he finished, Elizabeth's tree looked like a bandaged soldier who had just emerged from battle. "Well, that'll do for now," he said. "We'll see how they do next spring."

It was a long winter, and Elizabeth could hardly make herself look outside at the bandaged tree standing bravely in the yard. But when spring came, the tree began to blossom again. Not a lot of blossoms, mind you, but enough to show that the sap, the lifeblood, was flowing from the tree's healthy trunk into the branches again. And when summer came, the blossoms turned into small green apple buds. Grandfather stopped by to survey his handiwork.

"We'd better cut off those little apples, Elizabeth," he said, pulling out a sharp curved knife.

"No!" cried Elizabeth, but then stopped herself. "Why do you want to cut off the apples?" she asked.

"We can't put weight on the branches just yet," he answered lovingly. He tried one of the wrapped branches. "Not strong enough. Needs this year to heal up."

She nodded, understanding this time. "Can I do it?"

He handed her the knife with a smile. "You bet."

So one by one she removed the apple buds, knowing that she was sparing the branches by doing this. And when her birthday came, there was not one single apple on the tree. But the leaves were healthy and green, and the injured branches looked stronger. And after the frost Grandfather stopped by and helped her prune a few smaller branches, though not many.

By the following spring, the tree looked more beautiful than ever, just loaded with white blossoms. And when the apple buds came that summer, Grandfather said they could stay. And by Elizabeth's birthday there were enough big red apples to make at least a dozen pies, and lots of apple sauce, with plenty to share with her neighbors.

And after that, Elizabeth faithfully pruned her tree just like her grandfather had taught her. People came from miles around to admire her beautiful apple tree. And if they came on her birthday she even gave them a free apple! 🙟

THE TRUE VINE

Most of us don't know much about plants and trees and what it really takes to have them bear the most fruit they possibly can. When we want fruit or vegetables we head to the nearest store to buy what we need. So like Elizabeth we probably have little idea about pruning and how important it is to a plant.

But when Jesus lived, farming was very common. He often referred to trees and other plants when He wanted to teach an important lesson. He hoped to make things clear by speaking about things His listeners understood.

So when Jesus called Himself "The True Vine," people knew what He meant. They understood that a vine is the sturdy trunk of a plant that grows solidly from the ground, and it's the life source from which all the smaller branches spring forth. If the branches aren't healthy and well-connected to the vine, they shrivel and die and never produce any fruit. So Jesus used the grapevine to illustrate how important it is that we remain connected to Him.

He explained how we must stay attached to Him in order to remain alive and healthy—and to bear fruit! When we do, we bear the fruit of love, peace, joy, and much more—fruit we could never produce apart from Him. And it is fruit that is so colorful and appealing that others will notice there is something different about us.

But the fruit of the Spirit is love, joy, peace,

longsuffering, kindness, goodness, faithfulness, gentleness,

self-control. Against such there is no law.

GALATIANS 5:22-23 (NKJV)

OUR PRAYER

Dear Jesus, thank You for showing us how You're like a vine that gives life and nourishment to us, Your branches. Help us to remain tightly connected to You and to never let go. And we thank You in advance for all the fruit You will bring into our lives as we stay joined to You. Amen.

There's a stranger in town who sits by the well.

Why has He come? Can anyone tell?

He looks kind of tired, in need of a drink.

But why is He here? What do you think?

He says, "Those who thirst can come unto Me,

My water is living, and flows endlessly."

Who is this man? What's this about?

He is the Water that never runs out.

THE LIVING
WATER

"Whoever believes in me, as the

Scripture has said, streams of living water

will flow from within him."

JOHN 7:38 (NIV)

The Amazing Goatskin

Joshua and Michael knew they needed to make it across the desert before sunrise. After resting at an oasis during the heat of the day, they had filled their goatskin water bottles with fresh water. Then, just as the late afternoon air grew a little cooler, the two young men wearily started out on the last leg of their journey.

They traveled on foot, and soon their way was illuminated by the light of a three-quarter moon, everything around them transformed to varying shades of black and gray. Though a merciful evening breeze cooled the air, the reminder of the day's heat radiated up from the baked sand.

They knew this was the most dangerous leg of their three-day journey, this crossing of the tip of the great white desert. And they knew there was no room for mistakes or miscalculations if they hoped to reunite with their parents and family. They had carefully watched their landmarks—the rock shaped like a bundle of wheat and then the Joshua tree that showed the way to the oasis. And they had followed every single direction that old Uncle Jacob had written down for them on the parchment. The boys felt confident they would make it to the river by morning.

Michael, being the oldest, had led this expedition, but Joshua, having eyes like an eagle, had been the first to spot the landmarks along the way. Now Joshua kept an eye on the horizon as he followed his brother, and for some reason he felt they were moving off track.

"Michael," called Joshua, his voice sounding loud against the silence of the nighttime desert, "are you sure we're still on track?"

"Yes," returned Michael. "I'm watching the North Star, and we're just right."

Joshua didn't argue with him. He knew from experience it was senseless to argue with Michael, who was not only older, but bigger and stronger too. Besides, they needed to reserve every bit of energy to get them across this stretch of barren land, known to all as Dead Man's Crossing. So Joshua followed his brother, silently putting one foot in front of the other, concentrating only on keeping up, because he knew Michael's longer legs could carry him faster, and he didn't want to slow their travels down.

Then just when Joshua felt he couldn't lift his foot another step, he noticed a pale gray strip of light creeping up the eastern horizon. He wanted to shout and cheer but felt too tired to waste such energy, and so he just continued to plod along, imagining how wonderful that river would feel, how good that water would taste. He was so thirsty, his mouth felt like sand. They had long ago emptied their goatskins, and though relieved of the extra weight, his tongue felt like parchment. He had never known such thirst before!

Finally the sun rose above the horizon, illuminating the desert in shades of pink and rose. But something was wrong—they were still in the middle of the desert with nothing but desert in every direction. "Michael!" called Joshua with alarm. "Where are we?"

Michael stopped and looked around, perplexed. "I—I don't know. This doesn't look right."

Panic rushed through Joshua. To be caught in the desert like this was a slow and torturous death sentence. He shook his empty goatskin, then called our to his brother, "Do you have any water left? I'm all out now."

"Not a drop. I thought we'd be at the river by now."

Joshua's eyes searched the horizon for any possible source of water, finally spotting what appeared to be a large rock, possibly a place of shade and, if

Jehovah was watching over them, perhaps water. "There!" He pointed. "Let's go over to that rock."

This time Joshua led the way, going as fast as his legs would carry him, eager for shade and hoping beyond hope for water. When he reached the rock ahead of his brother, he found only a small wedge of shade, but he squatted in it, welcoming the temporary relief. He leaned his head against the coolness of the rock and prayed again for Jehovah's help. Then he began to feel and search around the rock, hoping to find even a small drop of condensation that he could lick with his tongue. But the rock was dry as old bones.

Then something shiny and brown caught his eye—it was a goatskin. A goatskin exactly like the one he carried. But it was full! He eagerly opened the spout and smelled the water to make sure it was good. His nose told him it was fine. So he took a sip. And it tasted better than fine—cool and fresh and so satisfying. He eagerly drank several more sips.

"What have you got there?" asked Michael, coming up from behind the rock.

Joshua looked up in surprise. And for a moment he considered lying and hiding the water from his brother. But instead he held it up. "Water! Jehovah has provided for us!"

"Where did you get that?" asked Michael.

"Right here. At this rock. I've been praying, and this must be Jehovah's way of helping us."

Michael scowled. "One goatskin of water?"

"One is better than none," offered Joshua.

Michael laughed in a mean way. "That will never get us across this desert."

Joshua scanned the horizon, looking to the north, the way they should be traveling, but he saw no familiar landmarks. "But we have no choice, Michael. We must continue." He handed the water to his brother. "Here, drink some, and then let's get going while it's still not too hot."

Michael took a long drink, then handed it back. "It's almost empty now. You finish it since you found it."

Then the two brothers began trekking north. Whenever Joshua got thirsty, he lifted the goatskin to his lips, expecting to get the last drop, but instead he would get a long drink. He offered Michael another drink.

"What? You still have water and you're willing to give it away, little brother?" Michael took a drink, then blinked in surprise. "Thanks. Now you finish the rest."

But every time Joshua had a drink, there seemed to be more water. And he continued to generously offer it to his brother, who was completely amazed. Finally Michael said, "You must be right, Joshua. This is no ordinary goatskin. Jehovah must've left this for us."

So they walked and walked, stopping frequently to drink the fresh, cool water from the goatskin. And by midday Joshua spotted a green line on the horizon. "That must be the river!" he shouted. And they began to walk faster, eager to cool themselves in its waters. Just as the river came into full sight, Joshua lifted up the goatskin for another drink. But now it was light and empty. He laughed and called out to his brother, "Jehovah has used this goatskin to keep us alive while crossing the desert, but now that we've reached the river, the water is gone."

"Blessed be the name of Jehovah!" shouted Michael. ✍

THE LIVING WATER

For many of us, water is something we take for granted. Most anytime we want it, it's available in ample supply. We drink it, wash with it, play in it, even waste it. And we probably never stop to think about how valuable water is to life.

But in the Middle East at the time Jesus lived on earth, water was sparse. There was no indoor plumbing, no faucets, no sprinklers, no hoses—just wells. And getting water home was hard work. Every morning someone had to trek to the well for a day's worth of water for drinking, washing, and cooking. They had to draw the water, pour it in jugs, and haul it home. That might take many trips. And the next day they would do it all over again. So when Jesus stopped by a village well and promised a woman Living Water that would never run out, He got His listener's attention, for water was precious.

But when Jesus spoke of Living Water, He wasn't referring to the kind that comes from a well. Instead, He was speaking of the water needed for the thirst within us—the thirst that comes from our souls and can only be quenched when we allow Jesus to pour Himself inside of us. The water He gives will wash us and fill us. It is the coolest, clearest, purest, most satisfying water ever! Spiritual refreshment that, like the goatskin in the desert, will never run dry!

Jesus replied, "If you only knew the gift God has for you and who I am, you would ask me, and I would give you living water."

JOHN 4:10 NLT

OUR PRAYER

Dear Jesus, thank You for being Living Water. Our souls so easily grow parched and thirsty. And only You can really quench and satisfy our hearts. So we invite You, once again, to fill us with Your cool, clean, refreshing Spirit who dwells inside us so that we too will never be thirsty again! Amen.

Who is this man? And why didi he come?

Was it for all? Or only for some?

How does the sunshine chase away night?

How does it cleanse the earth with its light?

Who is this man? What does He say?

"I'm the Light of the world. I am the way.

Just follow Me; don't walk in the night.

For I am the truth, and I am the Light!"

THE LIGHT OF THE WORLD

And Jesus spoke to them, saying,
"I am the light of the world. Whoever follows me
will never walk in darkness but will
have the light of life."

JOHN 8:12 (NRSV)

Follow the Light

❧ · ❧

One moonless winter evening, Rebekah's mother worked hard to finish weaving a blanket for Rebekah's cousin Mary who would be married the following day. Threads of blue and red and gold went in and out of the beautiful cloth. The yarns had been spun from the wool of her father's sheep, and Rebekah knew the blanket would be thick and warm and an honorable gift to present to her favorite cousin.

By the golden light from the big oil lamp, Rebekah watched with fascination as Mama's graceful fingers quickly worked the loom, sending the yarn back and forth—swish, swish, swish. But suddenly the room turned to darkness!

"What happened?" asked Rebekah.

"Oh, dear," said Mama. "The lamp is out of oil, and I'm afraid that was the very last drop of lamp oil too."

"Why is it so dark in here?" boomed Papa's voice, followed by a loud bang as he bumped into something.

"We're all out of lamp oil, Papa," cried Rebekah. "And Mama isn't finished with the wedding present yet."

Papa groaned. "And it's my fault because I forgot to buy lamp oil last week when I went to town."

"What will we do, Papa?" asked Rebekah. "It's too late to go to town. Besides, that would take all night, and the wedding is tomorrow." Usually Rebekah didn't mind that her family lived so far away from others. She enjoyed her freedom to roam the hills with the sheep and goats. But at moments like this she longed for a next-door neighbor. She looked out the window at the dark world that lay all about them, then suddenly remembered the old shepherd who lived way down the hill. "I could walk to Old Peter's!" she exclaimed. "I could borrow some lamp oil from him."

"Old Peter's?" laughed Papa. "Why, that's two miles away! How would you find your way in the dark? There isn't a moon or even any stars out tonight."

"Old Peter likes to read," explained Rebekah. "He might have his lamp burning, and I might see it."

"He might . . ." imitated Papa. "You might . . . But what if he has already gone to bed, and what if you get lost?"

"I won't get lost, Papa." Rebekah turned away from the window and tried to see her father in the house, but all she saw was blackness. "It's sure dark in here."

Papa laughed. "Yes, and it's dark out there. And it hasn't been all that long since you were afraid of the dark."

Rebekah considered this. "Yes, Papa, but now I know that God can see me even in the dark."

"Well," said Mama, "without lamp oil and light I will never be able to finish Mary's wedding gift in time, but . . . Although I appreciate your willingness, Rebekah, I don't like the idea of you going all by yourself in the dark."

"I agree," said Papa.

Rebekah's heart sank. "Then what will we do about Mary's wedding present?"

"I will go with you to Old Peter's," said Papa.

"Are you sure?" asked Rebekah. She knew her father was tired after caring for the goats and sheep all day, and he had gone many miles just to hunt down one particularly wayward goat.

"I am sure," said Papa. "We will be back as soon as we can, Mama."

And so Rebekah and Papa set off in the dark, trekking over the hills, he carrying a jug to hold the oil, and she carrying a small lantern that was also out of oil.

"Everything looks so different in the night," observed Rebekah with fear-tinged wonder.

"Yes," said Papa. "That's exactly why I was worried you might get lost."

"Why aren't you worried that you might get lost?"

Papa chuckled. "Well, I might, but I don't think so. I've roamed these hills since I was a boy."

Rebekah walked on ahead of Papa, testing herself to see how brave she was, and wondering if she really would've been able to make this trip through the darkness on her own. Then suddenly she spied it! Down the hill and a ways off, she could see the tiniest little spot of light.

"Look, Papa," she cried with delight. "There is Old Peter's hut, and I can see his light."

"You're right," said Papa. "And now, if you like, you may walk there all by yourself. Would you like that?"

Rebekah thought for a moment. She wasn't feeling as brave as she had earlier, but at the same time she knew Papa was tired. "Yes, Papa," she said. "You sit down here and wait, and I will return with the oil."

He handed her the jug, and she took off down the hill carrying both the lantern and the jug. Stepping carefully in the darkness, she kept her eyes on the light ahead of her, watching as it slowly, slowly grew bigger and brighter until she was standing right in front of the little shepherd's hut. "Old Peter!" she called from the front.

The door opened, and she was flooded in light. "Is that you, little Rebekah?" asked Old Peter. "What are you doing out all by yourself at night?"

She explained her errand and how Papa was waiting on the hill, and Old Peter filled her jug as well as her little lantern. "Now, let me light your lantern for you," he said.

She thanked him and headed back outside. It was nice having a lantern to light her way as she walked along. Especially since she was carrying the filled jug now, and she didn't want to take any chances of tripping and falling and breaking the jug. But as she began to climb the hill, she wasn't sure which direction to go. She thought she was going straight, but all she could see was pitch-black darkness before her. She turned to look back down at Old Peter's hut and was startled to see only darkness down there as well. *He must've gone to bed*, she said to herself as she continued up the hill. But with each additional step into the darkness, she began to feel more unsure. How was she to know she was going the right way? Papa might know these hills, but she wasn't as confident. Finally she stopped walking and cried out, "Papa! Where are you?"

"Up here," came his voice. "Keep walking to the right." And so she continued, calling out for reassurance as she went, until finally Papa was right before her, his big smile illuminated in the lamplight. "Good job, Rebekah."

"I was afraid I might not find you," she explained breathlessly. "It was easy finding Old Peter because I just followed the light. But coming back was hard because there was no light to follow."

Papa laughed. "Yes. If you hadn't been carrying that lantern, I couldn't have directed you. But because I could see you, I could tell you which way to walk."

"Oh, Papa," laughed Rebekah, "we would be so lost without the light!"

They continued home, and Mama was very happy to have her lamp oil. Tired from her nighttime walk, Rebekah went straight to bed. But when she got up the next morning, the first thing she saw was the beautiful blanket, all finished and sitting next to the window, its colors made brilliant by the morning light. Rebekah smiled as she ran her hand over Mama's fine handiwork. "Yes," she said happily, "we would be so lost without the light!" ❧

THE LIGHT OF THE WORLD

What an important lesson for us to learn: "We would be so lost without the light." Unless you have ever found yourself in a position like that of Rebekah and her family, you may take light for granted and not realize how important it is. But just turn off all the lights in your house tonight and shut the curtains tight—then you will understand how lost you would be without light.

The same thing is true for us spiritually. God's Word clearly shows us that without Christ we constantly live in spiritual darkness. Sin has blinded us to God's truth, and we are without light in our life. And yet God has given us an inner longing for light. Our hearts are drawn to it like a moth to a flame.

Still, as we draw near to Jesus' light, we see flaws in ourselves. His light exposes the ways we've blown it, things we'd rather hide. But at the same time it shows us the way we should go. His light illuminates our path so that we can follow Him with confidence.

And we desperately need the Light of the World. Only He can help us see ourselves as we truly are and can make us realize our need for forgiveness and salvation. He shines so that we no longer have to wander in the darkness but instead can rejoice in His light and His salvation! And in turn we reflect His light and shine forth God's truth to a lost world.

You are the light of the world—like a city on a mountain,

glowing in the night for all to see.

MATTHEW 5:14 NLT

OUR PRAYER

Dear Jesus, thank You for coming to earth to become the Light of the World. Thank You for shining your light of love and forgiveness into my heart. Help me to love Your light always, and to never try to hide in the darkness. For Your light is warmth and goodness and love! Amen.

Who is this child who sleeps in a manger?

Where is He from? Is He a stranger?

Why was He sent in the dark of the night?

Why does that star burn so pure and so bright?

Who is this child? What does He bring

To a hopeless world, unable to sing?

He's been sent down from heaven afar

To give to us hope—our Bright Morning Star!

THE BRIGHT MORNING STAR

"I, Jesus, have sent my angel to tell you

these things for the churches. I am the descendant

from the family of David, and I am

the bright morning star."

REVELATION 22:16 (NCV)

Hope in the Morning

❧ ∴ ☙

The physician removed his hand from Mama's hot forehead, then looked over at the young boy with a sad shake of his head. "Your mother is very ill, James," he said in a somber tone. "I won't lie to you, son. I seriously doubt that she will make it until morning."

"But she has to—" said James, fighting to hold back the tears. "She has to live—she's all I have in the whole world."

"I know." The doctor nodded as he packed up his instruments, then stood. "But there are good people in this village. Someone will take you in."

James looked down at the floor, shaking his head firmly. "I don't want anyone else. I want my mother to get better. I want her to live." He looked back at the doctor with pleading eyes. "Please tell me, isn't there anything I can do to help her?"

The doctor scratched his head. "Well, if you can hold down the fever . . . there have been a few times when I've seen a patient make it through this. You would need to keep her cool all night long by putting cool, wet towels on her. But you must understand, son, there is only a very small chance of her getting better."

But even a very small chance was enough to give James a glimmer of hope. And without even telling the doctor good-bye, he ran outside and refilled the jug with fresh, cool water, then immediately began soaking the cloths and placing them on his mother. And as soon as a cloth became warmed by the feverish heat from her body, he would replace it with another. Again and again and again.

Soon it was night, and he lit a small lantern, then continued his vigil, running outside every hour or so for cool water, never wanting to be away from her for more than a moment. He hoped he could keep this up throughout the night. But during this whole time, his mother never opened her eyes and never spoke a single word. She only moaned occasionally from the pain and fever that had taken hold of her body.

James had been caring for his mother for a full week before she had become so frighteningly ill that he'd gone out to find the physician. But during that whole week, he'd told himself that she would get well, that everything would be all right, and that God would surely not take his mother away when He'd just taken his father the year before.

But as the night grew dark and long and James became more and more exhausted, he began to wonder about whether anything he could do would help. Slowly his hope began to fade away, and he began to doubt himself and his ability to help his mother. Worse than that, he even began to doubt that God wanted to help.

He went outside once again and began to refill the water jug, pausing for a moment to glance up at the night sky. Hadn't this night been long enough? Shouldn't it be morning soon?

Then in an explosion of frustration and anger, he shook his fist at the inky black sky. "Are You even there, God?" he cried out. "Can You even see me? Do You even hear me? Will this night ever end?" Then he just broke down and sobbed. For several minutes he cried and cried. When he could cry no more he looked up again, and for some reason he felt a tiny spark of hope.

"Dear God, please forgive me for doubting You," he said. "But I really need Your help right now. Please, I beg You, please help my mother make it through the night. And then make her well again." That was all he could make himself say; he just hoped God would answer.

Then he hurried back into the house, and for what felt like the thousandth time he dipped a cloth into the cool water, then wrung it out and gently laid it across his mother's forehead. "Come on, Mama," he whispered, "just make it until morning. Just until morning, and then you'll feel better."

Again and again throughout that long night he looked out the window, longing like he'd never longed before to see the morning star that would signal the coming dawn. Oh, if only it would come soon.

He studied his mother by the lantern's soft light. Her face seemed more relaxed now, more peaceful. But he wasn't so sure that was a good sign. Some people said death was peaceful, and he surely didn't want her to die. So he kept on working steadily, continuing to place and replace the cool, wet cloths on his mother's forehead, silently praying for strength and silently hoping for morning to come.

And then, just when he felt he could neither lift nor wring one more cloth, when his arms and hands felt like they were made of stone, when all he wanted to do was to close his eyes and sleep, sleep, sleep . . . just then he saw his mother's eyes open. She slowly turned her head and looked out the window. And then she smiled.

He turned to see what it was she saw, and there, balanced on the edge of the eastern horizon, was a small, perfect star. A star filled with hope and promise and light and life. The bright morning star had finally come!

And following that star came the first rays of the sun, and somehow in that moment James knew he had done everything earthly possible to make it through that long and hopeless night, and then God had stepped in and carried him until morning.

His mother reached out and placed a weak hand on his arm, then smiled and said, "Morning's here."

"Yes." James sighed with relief. "And hope is here too."

James's mother recovered completely, and they enjoyed a long healthy life together. And when James grew up, he studied medicine and became an excellent and much-loved doctor. But what his patients appreciated most about him was the way he always brought hope into their lives. And he was often quoted as saying, "Hope is like that bright morning star that always comes after the longest and darkest night." ❧

THE BRIGHT MORNING STAR

There is something about the night that makes a bad situation seem much, much worse. Whether it's a loved one being ill, a storm howling outside, or just being all alone in a strange place, the dark of night somehow makes things seem even more dismal than they are. And if you have ever had one of those nights, you know how glad you were when morning finally came. Somehow the light of day brightens our spirits and gives us new hope.

It is interesting to realize that the name Bright Morning Star is used for

Jesus only one time in all of Scripture. It is even more interesting that it appears in the last chapter of the last book of the Bible ever written. Once the apostle John completed his writing, God would be through speaking to us directly. In fact, the next time we will hear right from God Himself is when He calls His children home to heaven. But in some of the last words from God He calls His Son the Bright Morning Star.

Now why did He use that name? It could be He knew that in a world so darkened by sin His children would feel as though the night would never end. Out of love He knew we would need a reminder that the night can't last forever. And so He proclaimed that His Son was the Bright Morning Star—the one whose coming again would bring a new day of hope and promise. In our dark world we need not fear the night, because the day is coming when our Bright Morning Star will shine His light for all to see.

Looking for the blessed hope and the glorious appearing
of our great God and Savior, Christ Jesus.

TITUS 2:13 (NKJV)

OUR PRAYER

Dear God, thank You for sending Jesus to be our hope, our Bright Morning Star. Help us to keep our eyes and our spiritual compasses fixed on Him, and to keep His hope alive in our hearts. Even when it feels like the night is long, help us to remember that morning is coming! Amen.

Who is this man, so gentle, so kind,

Who heals the lepers, the lame, and the blind,

Who loves all the children and also the poor?

Why is He here? What is He for?

What makes this man so calm and so pure?

He teaches us love—will His lessons endure?

He rules all in peace, and not with a rod.

Our great sacrifice—the Lamb of God.

THE LAMB OF GOD

*The next day he [John the Baptist]
saw Jesus coming toward him and declared,
"Here is the Lamb of God who takes
away the sin of the world!"*

JOHN 1:29 (NRSV)

The Best Dog

❧ ⋅ ❧

Thomas couldn't actually recall a time when Shep hadn't been around. They had grown up together. He remembered playing with Shep when they were almost the same size, and then he remembered the nights when he'd been afraid of the dark and Shep had kept him company, and the time he'd been sick and Shep had stayed right by his side until he got better. Yep, Shep was a good dog all right.

And although Father had a number of excellent sheepdogs, always training one or the other, there was no doubt in Thomas's mind that Shep was top dog and the favorite of the whole family.

And despite the fact that Shep was getting on in years, he still remained just as fast and smart as ever—Thomas was willing to bet on it. In fact, just about everybody around agreed that Shep was the best sheepdog ever. Thomas's father had been offered lots of money for Shep again and again. But each time he just shook his head and said, "Nope. Selling Shep would be like selling one of my own children." And Thomas, the youngest child, agreed with his father wholeheartedly. Shep was almost as good as a little brother, and he and the dog were the best of friends.

Now in the summer when Thomas was finally old enough to take care of the sheep by himself (with the help of Shep, of course), he and the dog spent even more time together. Each day they worked together moving the flock from field to field.

Toward the end of that summer Thomas and Shep prepared to herd the small flock of sheep up to one of the highest portions of his family's land for a week.

"Now, you're sure you're ready to do this, son?" his father asked as Thomas rechecked his provisions.

Thomas looked straight into his father's eye (he could do this since he was almost as tall as him now) and answered, "Yep, I know I can handle this." Then he reached over and scratched Shep's ear with a grin. "And if I can't, well, you can be sure Shep here can."

Father nodded. "Okay. You two are an excellent team, and I'm not worried. The flock's in good hands."

Thomas agreed. He and Shep knew just what to do to drive the sheep up the hills and keep them all together. Actually Shep did most of the work, but he followed the commands Thomas gave him. Father had taught Thomas all those signals long ago when he was still a small boy. And today Thomas felt confident that he and Shep could handle whatever adventures might lie ahead. In Shep's more than a dozen years of working sheep, he'd never lost a single one—a proud record for any shepherd, whether dog or man.

They reached the high meadow just before sundown, and Shep and Thomas had no trouble bedding the tired sheep down for the night. Thomas stretched out on his bedroll and looked up at the stars. This would be a fine week.

For the first few days everything went just as smooth as honey on a hot summer's day. The sheep, glad to be in a cooler place, were content to graze from the green meadow and drink from the cold mountain stream. Sometimes Thomas wondered if they even needed a shepherd to watch over them.

Until the fifth night.

On that night, after the sheep were quieted down, Shep became unusually uneasy. "What is it, boy?" asked Thomas as he watched Shep pacing back and forth around the edge of the resting flock. Shep looked at Thomas, then on up toward the rough mountain terrain above them. And that's when Thomas heard it too. The faint and distant sound of wolves. "They sound pretty far off, Shep," said Thomas reassuringly. "But just to be safe, I'll throw a couple more logs on the fire and stay up to keep watch with you."

He built up the fire, then leaned against a rock, eyes and ears wide open, shepherd's staff close by. But after a while his eyelids grew heavy, and soon he fell fast asleep.

But he awoke with a start, the urgent sounds of Shep's barking filling his ears. He grabbed his staff and ran toward the sound of the commotion just in time to see Shep fighting off the attack of three vicious wolves, two going after Shep, and the other already yelping and running the other direction. Thomas picked up several large stones and pelted one of the wolves, yelling and screaming as he did so. He could hear the frightened flock scrambling behind him, but there was no time to try to calm them now. He picked up more stones and hurled them at the attacking wolves. One hit a wolf right on the nose so hard he ran off yelping. But one wolf, the largest of the three, remained.

Now that beast and Shep were wildly fighting—rolling and snarling and biting. Thomas continued to yell but was afraid to throw any stones for fear of hurting Shep. So he ran toward the scuffle, his shepherd's staff raised in his hand and yelling as loudly as he could, "Get out of here, you mangy old wolf! Get him, Shep! Get him good!" And then finally Shep had the wolf pinned, about to go for the beast's throat, but somehow the wolf escaped and took off for the hills.

"Good job, Shep!" screamed Thomas with joy as he ran to Shep's side. "You're the greatest!" But just as he got there, Shep collapsed to the ground. "Shep?" cried Thomas as he knelt by the injured dog. "Are you all right, boy?"

Thomas gently gathered the large dog in his arms and carried him over to the light of the fire, tenderly laying him down on his own bedroll. "Shep?" he pleaded as he gently stroked the dog's head, now wet with blood. "You gotta be all right, boy." He quickly checked the dog's wounds, using his own clothing to try to stop the bleeding. But he knew enough about farming and animals to know that the wound at Shep's neck was very serious. "Oh, Shep!" he cried as he buried his face in the dog's furry coat. "Please don't die, boy. You're the best friend I've got. You're the best dog ever!"

Shep moved his head slightly as his warm tongue licked Thomas's hand for one last time, as if to say good-bye. And then the dog grew completely still and quiet. Thomas knew his friend was gone, and his own tears poured freely over Shep's warm coat. Behind him he could still hear the frightened sheep stirring, and as much as he hated to leave his dog, he knew his job was to care for his sheep.

It was the longest night of his life, but Thomas finally got the sheep settled down and the fire built up, and he continued to keep watch, afraid the wolves might return. But apparently Shep had thoroughly frightened the beasts, and they didn't come back. At first light, Thomas wrapped Shep in his bedroll. Then, carrying the dog, he drove the sheep back down the hill and home.

Mother and Father both cried when they heard the news. And Father helped Thomas dig a grave and bury their old friend. On the marker Thomas wrote the simple words, "Shep, the Best Dog Ever," and Mother laid a bouquet of her best roses on the grave. Then Father spoke a few words. "There's not a braver or better way for a good sheepdog to die than to lay down his life protecting his sheep. And that's what Shep did. We will remember him always."

And later that day something special happened that became a constant reminder of good old Shep. Molly, another fine sheepdog, had six puppies. And the biggest and strongest one they named Shep, after his daddy.

THE LAMB OF GOD

Stories like this one usually bring tears to our eyes. It makes us sad to think that such a great animal would have to give up its life for others. You might feel different if Shep were a mangy, old, ornery mutt, but he wasn't. He was the best dog—and friend—a boy could ever have. And so we are moved by his sacrifice.

But the idea of an animal sacrificing its life for others is not something new. Just pick up your Bible and turn all the way back to Exodus 12. There you will read about another animal that had to give its life to save others—the Passover lamb. And the lamb that God required was not some old, worn-out, ornery sheep. God asked for the very best lamb of all to be sacrificed. The lamb had to be spotless and healthy and strong. And this lamb was to be killed and its blood put on the doorposts of the house to bring God's salvation.

So when Jesus was called "the Lamb of God," do you realize what that meant? By taking on that name He was saying, "I will make the ultimate sacrifice. I will give My life so others can live." So when you stop and think about Christ's sacrifice, how do you feel? Just think, the very Son of God, the one who was perfect in every way, gave His life so that we can live. In some ways we should be saddened by the thought. But in other ways we should rejoice in the fact that Jesus loved us enough to become "the Lamb of God who takes away the sin of the world!"

But he paid for you with the precious lifeblood of Christ,

the sinless, spotless Lamb of God.

1 PETER 1:19 (TLB)

OUR PRAYER

Dear God, thank You so much for sending Jesus to be the final sacrifice for our sins. Thank You, Jesus, for Your willingness to come to earth to suffer and endure a painful and humiliating death for our sakes, and for spilling Your blood in order that we might have eternal life. Help us to never take Your death lightly or for granted. Amen.

Who is this man, what is He for?

If He's a lion, when will He roar?

Did He come down to rule as the king

Over all Israel, their freedom to bring?

Who is this man, what's He about?

Why do the leaders scream and cry out?

This is the One who's sent from above,

To rule in our hearts, the Lion of Love.

THE LION
OF JUDAH

Then one of the elders said to me,
"Do not weep! See, the Lion of the tribe of Judah,
the Root of David, has triumphed. He is able
to open the scroll and its seven seals."

REVELATION 5:5 (NIV)

The True King

❧∴❧

Young Jack, though very smart, was too poor to attend school like most of the boys his age. Instead he stayed home and helped his grandmother by delivering the clothing that she sewed and mended each day.

"Times weren't always like this, Jack," said Grandma one day.

"What happened to change things?" asked Jack.

"Well, long ago—" she paused. "Or maybe it just seems long ago—anyway, we had a good king, a true king!"

"A true king?" asked Jack. "Isn't King Frederick a true king?"

She shook her head, then in a low voice said, "No. King Frederick only pretends to be the true king. But at least he's not as bad as his brother King Harold!"

"Yes," said Jack, "I've heard King Harold was horribly mean and cruel. King Frederick is better, I suppose, although he's not very kind or good to the people."

"That's because he's not a true king," added Grandma.

"But what makes a true king?" asked Jack.

Her eyes got a faraway look. "You've got to be born into it, Jack. Now, dear King John, he was a true king."

Jack smiled. "Yes, I've heard tales of him."

Grandma's eyes grew frightened. "Who has told you of King John? It's very dangerous to speak of him!"

"It's okay," Jack said as he patted her hand. "I was told in secret. Old

70
❧

Henry tells me lots of things, but I've promised to keep everything a secret. You know, he was a close friend of King John."

Grandma sighed in relief. "Old Henry is a good man, and very wise. One day he will tell you all of the truth."

"All of the truth?" asked Jack.

Grandma smiled. "Yes, when you are older."

"Old Henry has told me many fine tales of King John," said Jack. "But I never heard what happened to him."

She shuddered. "It was tragic. That horrible King Harold and his men stormed the castle one night." She let out a sob. "They killed the entire royal family. Only the tiny infant, who was hidden, survived."

"What happened to the baby?"

Her voice grew hushed. "He was rescued by his old nanny. But he is a boy now. And someday, when the time is just right, he will reclaim the kingdom."

Jack nodded. "Then everyone in the kingdom will be happy again." Although the people couldn't talk about it, Jack knew how badly they all longed for change.

"Yes, for when the True King reveals himself, he will also unlock the box that contains the True Rules."

Jack fingered the old key that hung around his neck on a golden chain. It had been there for as long as he could remember. "Grandma?" he asked curiously. "You always tell me this key is for when I get older. But what will it unlock? Does it have anything to do with—"

"Hush now," she said quietly, but she smiled warmly at him. "The day is coming when all shall be made known."

In the next few years Jack grew older and taller, and despite not going to school he grew much wiser (thanks to Old Henry). And finally the day came when Old Henry told Jack a most amazing secret. "You have heard me speak often of King John," began Old Henry. "As you know, he was my good friend, and the True King. But what you don't know is that he was also your father."

Jack almost fell over. "King John was my father?"

"Yes. And the time will come when you must step up to the throne. The kingdom has suffered dearly these past years. But I have taught you all that I know—everything I learned while serving your kind father."

Jack felt too stunned to speak. He had suspected something unusual before. But that he was the son of the great King John, the True King . . . ! Finally he spoke. "But how will I know when it's time? And what will I do?"

"You are the son of the True King, Jack. And when the time comes, trust me, you'll know."

Jack kept this news to himself, continuing life as he'd always done—working for his grandmother, helping people in need, trying to cheer the downhearted. Then one day he overheard a commotion in the street (not unusual in their unhappy kingdom), and he ran to see if he could help out.

"Get this wretched old woman out of my sight at once!" yelled King Frederick to his royal guard. With disgust, he pointed to the poor widow begging on the corner. "Such useless riffraff have no place in my kingdom!"

"Wait!" cried Jack, stepping between the royal guards and the frightened woman. "Please, let her be. She can come home and stay with my grandmother!"

"How dare you!" screamed the king, his face twisted in rage. "Guards, arrest this foolish young pup!"

The gathering crowd, many of them friends of Jack, all gasped. And then Old Henry stepped forward. "Stop!" he called in a loud voice. "You cannot arrest this young man."

"Why not?" demanded the king with narrowed eyes.

And then with confidence Jack spoke up. "Because I am the True King."

Now everyone gasped even louder. Staring at Jack with wide eyes, they began to whisper among themselves.

"Impossible!" growled the king. "I am the king."

"Not the True King," said Old Henry in a calm but firm voice. "Let's go to the castle so he can prove his claim."

"I'll arrest you both!" screamed the king.

But the guards didn't move (for they too had been waiting for the True King). Then the people began to shout out, demanding that Jack be given a chance to prove himself. And soon they all pressed around and began to move in one mass toward the castle.

In the castle courtyard, the infuriated king grabbed Jack by the collar. "Prove that you are king!" he demanded

"Bring out the rules!" cried Old Henry.

Soon an ornate box, blackened by smoke, was brought and set before the king. Everyone stared in wonder.

"Everyone knows that only the True King can open that box," said Old Henry. "Can you open it, King Frederick?"

The king snarled and shook his head. Then Jack reached down beneath his shirt, and the crowd gasped when they saw him hold up the beautiful golden key.

Jack slipped the key into the lock. And of course it worked! Then he reached into the box and pulled out a scroll. Unrolling it, he read in a loud voice, "'The Rules of the True Kingdom: The first is to love God. The second is to love your neighbor.'" He smiled. "And so it shall be."

The guards immediately seized King Frederick and took him to the dungeon, while everyone else cheered, "Long live the True King! Long live the True King! Long live King Jack!" ❧

THE LION OF JUDAH

The only time in all of Scripture that Jesus is called the Lion of the tribe of Judah is in Revelation 5. In this chapter the scene is heaven, and the call has gone out for someone to come and open the book sealed with seven seals. As all of heaven and earth awaits, no one steps forward. Apparently no one is worthy enough to answer the call. At that prospect John begins to weep. What will happen if no one comes forward?

But then we discover that there is one who is worthy—one who has the power and authority to open the book. It is Jesus Himself. The one whom many consider to be merely a kind man or a moral teacher or a religious leader reveals who He really is—just like Jack revealed himself as king.

At that moment it becomes clear to all that the submissive Lamb of God who willingly laid down His life on the cross is the same Lion of Judah who has the power and strength to accomplish what no one else can. For Jesus is the Son of God. He is the one who spoke a word, and the universe was created. He is the Sovereign Lord of heaven and earth. He is our True King. Just like many were surprised the day Jack showed himself as king, so too will many be in awe when Jesus stands before them as the Lion of Judah. And for those who know the Lion and have let Him rule in their lives, it will be a great day of rejoicing.

And being found in appearance as a man,

He humbled Himself and became obedient to the point of death,

even the death of the cross. Therefore God also has highly exalted Him

and given Him the name which is above every name, that at the name of

Jesus every knee should bow, of those in heaven, and of those on earth,

and of those under the earth, and that every tongue should confess

that Jesus Christ is Lord, to the glory of God the Father.

PHILIPPIANS 2:8-11 (NKJV)

OUR PRAYER

Dear God, thank You so much for sending Jesus to be the Lion of Judah—not so He could rule over Israel, but so He could rule over the whole universe, for all eternity. And so He could rule and reign in my very own heart. I acknowledge Jesus as the True King of my heart. Amen.

Who is this man with staff in His hand?

Leading the sheep? I don't understand!

To wander the hills, to find what is lost,

What is it for? What does it cost?

Who is this man who cares for His sheep,

Leads them to water, watches them sleep?

He says He loves me and that I'm His lamb.

He's the Good Shepherd, the Great I Am.

THE GOOD
SHEPHERD

"I am the good shepherd.

The good shepherd gives His life for the sheep."

JOHN 10:11 (NKJV)

The Shepherd's Heart

When Samuel was just a little boy, he would beg and beg to go out with his father to help look after the sheep. "Soon enough you will be out here," his father would say. "The time to work will come before you know it."

So while his father was off caring for the sheep out on the rolling hills, Samuel would find a tall stick and pretend to be a shepherd with Mama's chickens. But chickens can be stubborn and flighty creatures, and it was no easy task to herd them along. Still, Samuel thought it was good practice for being a shepherd.

Finally the day came when Samuel was old enough to go with his father. He was so full of excitement, he could hardly sleep the night before. He couldn't wait to carry the little staff Papa had made for him and to herd those sheep along to the high grassy places.

Early the next morning, Samuel was dressed and ready to go. He told Mama good-bye and then walked with Papa out to the big meadow where they began gathering up their small flock of sheep and driving them up to the cooler high places where the summer grass still grew green and lush. For the whole day he walked at the rear of the herd, making sure none of the slower ewes or little lambs went astray. By evening, after they had settled down the sheep for the night, Samuel was very, very tired and fell quickly and soundly asleep.

But in the middle of the night, Samuel bolted awake! He wasn't even sure what had interrupted his sleep, but he sat quietly for a moment just listening to the still night sounds all around him, and then he heard it again—that faint and far-off noise that had awakened him. He strained his ears to listen to what sounded like the distant bleating of a lamb. A lamb in trouble!

Samuel glanced around their camp bathed in soft moonlight, but Papa and all the other sheep were fast asleep. None seemed troubled by the sound, and he wondered if maybe he had only imagined it or perhaps even dreamed it. He started to lay back down, tired after the long day's work. But then the sound came again, faint but very real.

He stood up, picked up his shepherd's staff, and then began to walk in the direction of the sound, pausing every so often to listen again just to be sure he was still going the right way. As he walked he wondered why the lamb had decided to wander off at night. Didn't it know what kind of dangers lurked out in the darkness? Samuel remembered some of the exciting stories Papa often told in the wintertime. Stories about bears, lions, and wolves, all trying to get themselves a little lamb for their late-night dinner. And suddenly Samuel began to feel a little worried. A bear or lion might also like to eat a young boy who was wandering around after dark—a boy without a single weapon, other than his small staff, with which to protect himself.

Samuel stopped in his tracks and looked back at the campsite where the fire still burned, although it only looked like a small red spot to him from here. Then he heard that bleating sound again, much closer now. The lamb was clearly in trouble. Still, Samuel wasn't so sure he wanted to go head to head with a lion or a bear or a wolf. And now he felt torn. A frightened voice within him whispered that he should return to camp, pretend like he'd heard nothing, and get a good night's sleep. But a stronger voice encouraged him to continue on and find the endangered lamb.

"Dear God," he prayed as he began to walk steadily toward the sound of the frightened lamb, "please help me because I am feeling very, very scared."

He continued on, then stopped for a moment to pick up some stones to put in his pocket, just in case. He'd heard stories of another shepherd who had defended himself and his sheep with a well-thrown stone. Although Samuel wasn't the best shot, he was willing to try if needed. He continued on, the sound of the lamb's cries growing louder and closer.

"God is with me," he said quietly with each step. "God is with me."

Finally he reached the place where he had to climb over some rocks, and he wondered how a little lamb possibly could have climbed over them. Or had a larger animal carried it? For a brief moment he considered turning back again. But then he shook his head and climbed bravely over the rocks with a stone in one hand and his staff in the other, certain he would soon come face to face with something big and wild and frightening—something snarling and angry with large, sharp teeth!

But when he got over the top of the rocks, he saw no wild animal. No bear, no lion, not even a wolf. All he saw was a frightened little lamb, his small hoof wedged between two stones.

"Hello, little one," called Samuel as he quickly approached the troubled lamb. "What have you gotten yourself into here?" Then he gently worked with the little leg until it was finally free from its rocky trap. "How's that?" he asked, and the lamb let out what sounded like a happy bleat and wobbled toward him. But Samuel could tell by the lamb's limp that his leg was hurt.

And so he bent down and gently picked up the lamb, then struggled to carefully arrange the lamb over his shoulders the same way he'd seen his father do, front legs over one side, back legs over the other. But it looked much easier when his father did it. Still, the lamb cooperated with his fumbling, probably relieved to be rescued.

Then Samuel turned and headed back to camp, speaking quietly and reassuringly to the lamb as he went. "You should never wander away like that, little one," warned Samuel. "Don't you know you could end up being dinner for a hungry lion or bear?"

The lamb gave a little bleat as if he understood. Samuel continued, "Your shepherd cares about you and doesn't want you to go out and get hurt. And if you stick with your shepherd you'll have all the things you need. Things like good grass and clean water. But best of all you'll have protection from enemies that would try to hurt you."

Back at the camp, Samuel eagerly bedded down again, tucking the little lamb right in beside him. When he awoke the next morning his father was standing over him, his face amused. "What's this?" he said.

Samuel explained about his late-night search for the lamb, and his father smiled and said, "Yes, it's very clear you are cut out for this kind of work, son. For it's plain to see you have a shepherd's heart."

Samuel nodded, pretending to understand his father's comment, but it wasn't until many, many years later that he came to fully appreciate the meaning of his father's high praise. ❧

THE GOOD SHEPHERD

Have you ever had someone ask you what kind of animal you'd like to be? Have you ever answered, "I want to be a sheep"? Probably not. That's because sheep aren't really that special. Just think about it. Sheep aren't very fast like horses or cheetahs or dolphins. They aren't very strong and brave like lions or tigers or bears. They aren't very smart like foxes or monkeys or owls. They are timid, defenseless, and not very bright—not really the kind of animal anyone would want to be.

Then it's no wonder that sheep are so dependent on their shepherd. They count on him for everything—food, water, shelter, safety. What's really interesting, though, is that when God chose to compare us to an animal, He decided to call us sheep. And like all sheep, we need a Shepherd.

You see, each of us is like the lamb in the story who wandered off and got himself in big trouble. We are lost. We are in danger. And we are unable to get back to safety. But Jesus is the Good Shepherd. He said that He came to seek and save those who were lost. And he proved it by giving His life for His sheep. Without Him as our shepherd we would all be in big trouble. But He promised that if we call out to Him and trust in Him, He will take care of us. What a great promise from the Good Shepherd!

"For this is what the Sovereign Lord says: I myself will search and find my sheep. I will be like a shepherd looking for his scattered flock. I will find my sheep and rescue them from all the places to which they were scattered on that dark and cloudy day."

EZEKIEL 34:11-12 (NLT)

OUR PRAYER

Dear Jesus, we thank You for being our Good Shepherd. We thank You for giving us all we need, for protecting us from what would hurt us, and for leading us safely through this life—and finally home to be with You. Amen.

Who is this man with thorny crown,

Dressed in rags, stumbling down?

Beaten, despised—treated like dirt,

Pain in His eyes—how He must hurt.

Who is this man, mocked by the crowd

As they hurl insults, jeering out loud?

Yet He forgives, trades hatred for love—

The King of all kings sent down from Above.

KING OF KINGS

"These will wage war against the Lamb, and the Lamb will overcome them, because He is Lord of lords and King of kings, and those who are with Him are the called and chosen and faithful."

REVELATION 17:14 (NASB)

The King's Secret

❦ · ❧

In the land of Bibbidi, the rulers always came from one family, mainly because that family owned the castle and all the surrounding land, and it seemed right that they should take care of things. But they were a good family and had ruled the people fairly. And for many years no one complained. But King Bibbidi the Twelfth thought it would be wise to appoint a council and listen to the people he ruled.

So he carefully chose three upstanding citizens and named them to his council. But while they presented many good questions, they provided little in the way of answers. Nevertheless, they got him thinking as they told him about problems with poor people, the jail system, litter, and a number of other things.

"Goodness," said King Bibbidi the Twelfth as he scratched his head. "And I thought the kingdom was running so smoothly. Why didn't I hear about these problems before?"

"No one wants to trouble the good king with these kinds of problems," offered the first councilman.

"Yes," said another. "Whenever the king passes by, everyone tries to make everything look perfect and fine."

"That's right," agreed the third. "Your people love you; they don't want to upset you with their concerns."

"Hmmm," said the king, thinking about all he'd just heard and wondering how he could find out more. Being a smart king, he soon arrived at a solution. And being a wise king, he kept his idea to himself.

A few days later he told his three council members, "I can see you're all very concerned about making the kingdom better. Unfortunately, that will have to wait, for I have some pressing business to take care of in a far-off land. But I am sure the kingdom will be safe in your care." Then he signed a royal decree giving the council authority until his return. And with that he got into his royal carriage and rode out of town. Then he climbed from the carriage and told his faithful driver to continue to the far-off region and stay there until sent for.

Then the king stepped behind some bushes, removed his royal clothing, and replaced it with poor man's attire, rubbing a little dirt on his hands and face to complete the disguise. He hid his clothing, keeping only his royal ring tucked safely in his pocket. Then he headed back into town on foot. Several wagons passed him by, and no one offered him a ride. He didn't mind so much, for this was a new and exciting experience for him. However, by the time he reached town late that afternoon, his feet were blistered and sore, and he was very hungry.

He knocked on a neat cottage door, just on the outskirts of town, offering to work for food, but he was quickly turned away. He tried another and then another, but each time was turned away. Finally he reached the town square with the castle nearby, and there he sat on a bench.

"You can't sit there," declared a guard.

"Why not?" asked the king.

"No tramps allowed."

"I'm not a tramp," said the king.

"You have a job then? A place to live?"

"I just arrived in town, and I've found no work yet."

"Then you're a tramp, and you'd best leave if you know what's good for you."

The king rose slowly to his feet, looking at the dirty streets all around. "If I work hard cleaning the streets, can I stay?"

The guard shrugged. "Maybe."

So the king began to pick up the junk and debris that littered the town square. He worked diligently until dark, then sat back down on the bench, his stomach rumbling with hunger. He looked around at the dwellings of his people. Most homes looked cozy and nice, but some appeared quite poor. Just as he studied one particularly shabby looking little shack, the door opened and an old bent-over woman came out and hobbled over to his bench.

"I sees you a picking up out here," she said, "and I thinks you must be good. So I brings you a little bit a soup and a little bit a bread. T'ain't much, but 'tis all I can spare."

He smiled and thanked her. "Can you sit and visit with me a little?" She nodded, then sat down. As he ate his meager meal, he asked about her life, how she made her living, what things she'd like to see changed.

"You's a curious man," she finally said after answering all of his questions. "You looks like a tramp, but you talks like a scholar."

He nodded. "Yes, and you look like a poor woman, but you have a kind heart."

"Well, you takes care," she said as she headed for her home. "And mind you, watch out for the soldiers."

That night the king slept on the bench. Actually, he hardly slept at all. He was too busy thinking about all the changes he wanted to make to better the kingdom. And besides, the bench was hard and cold. But when he awoke, it was to the bright morning sun and a sharp jab in the ribs. "Get up, you!" demanded a guard. "On your feet!"

The king stood, barely awake, and the guard quickly bound his hands and pushed him toward the prison gates. "I told you last night, no tramps allowed!"

Before he knew it, the king was thrown right into prison. He'd never seen the prison this close before and was appalled at the filth and cruelty he found there. He questioned prisoners about the conditions and why they were there. Some, like him, had been treated unfairly.

"Guard!" he called with authority. "Come at once!"

The guard walked over and sneered. "What d' ya want, yer highness?"

"Good," said the king, "you recognize me—"

"Ha!" the guard laughed "Recognize you? I've never seen you in my life. You're just a good-for-nothing tramp."

"No," he said, "I am King Bibbidi the Twelfth." His hands still bound, he couldn't reach into his pocket for the ring, and the guard laughed even harder.

"And I'm St. Nicholas," he snarled. "Now be quiet!"

The king blinked in surprise, then stepped back and wondered what to do next. He tried to talk to the other prisoners, explaining why he was there, but they just turned their backs to him, treating him like a madman, a lunatic.

Then more guards came. Roughly they grabbed him, dragging him back to the street. "You'll find out what we do with lying impostors who claim to be our king!" And they stood him up before his three council members, charging him with impersonating their king.

"But I am your king," he pleaded. "Listen!"

"See?" said the mean guard. "There he goes again."

"As the law states, you must beat him soundly and then throw him out of town," said the lead council member.

"You must heed me," shouted the king in his most kingly, royal voice. "My insignia ring is in my shirt pocket."

"Check his pocket," directed a council member.

The guard reached in, then produced the royal ring, and the crowd gasped. "I am your king!" shouted the monarch with authority as his hands were freed. Then he removed his cap and wiped his face, and all his people bowed before him. "And now I know what it is like to be one of the lowliest of my subjects." He glanced over at the mean guard. "And believe me, some things are going to change around here!" ✎

KING OF KINGS

What a surprise it must have been for everyone to realize that the tramp who was about to be beaten was really the king of the land. It would not have been a good day to be one of the council members—or the mean guard. If they had only looked at him more carefully, if they had only listened to what he said, maybe, just maybe they would have recognized who he was. But they had already made up their minds; to them he was just a tramp.

More than 2,000 years ago, when the King of kings walked this earth, His chosen people treated Him no better. Jesus' life clearly showed that He was the promised Messiah; yet few bothered to look at Him closely enough to understand who He was. He told them plainly why He had come; yet they refused to listen to what He had to say. They'd made up their minds. To them

He was an impostor, a liar, a lunatic. They refused to acknowledge Him as their king and as King of kings. So what did they do? They killed Him.

But that didn't change who He was. Just because people don't recognize a king when they see him doesn't make him less of a king. Three days later Jesus rose from the grave. He conquered sin and death, and He proved once and for all that He is the King of kings. Only one question remains: Will you reject Him like others who refused to see who He is, or will you acknowledge and embrace Him as King of kings—and King of your life? Like all who have gone before you, it's your choice. What will it be?

And He has on His robe and on His thigh a name written:
KING OF KINGS AND LORD OF LORDS.

REVELATION 19:16 (NKJV)

OUR PRAYER

Dear Jesus, precious Son of God, thank You for leaving all the glories and comforts of heaven to come down to earth to be treated so cruelly, so unjustly. Thank You that You loved us so much that You were willing to endure all that You suffered just so we could live with You forever in heaven. We humbly acknowledge that You are, and always have been, the King of all kings, and the King of our hearts. Amen.

Who is this man who speaks about bread?

He says He is food and that we will be fed.

We won't go hungry if we just believe

That He can give us all that we need.

Who is this man? How can He be

The food that will stop the hunger in me?

He wants to fill me, to take away strife,

To meet every need—He's the Bread of Life.

THE BREAD
OF LIFE

Jesus replied, "I am the bread of life.
No one who comes to me will ever be hungry again.
Those who believe in me will never thirst."

JOHN 6:35 (NLT)

Daily Bread

❧ · ❧

Times were hard in Rachel's small village. Spring rains never came, and the summer's hot winds dried what little crops had managed to survive until every grainfield, for as far as Rachel could see, was a dusty, dry tan color. And everyone in the village worried and fretted over this horrible drought, talking of little else. "We will have no bread to eat," said a young woman as she drew a bucket of water from the village well. Rachel waited for the woman to move away, and then she began to draw water for her family, listening, as always, to the daily chatter of the women.

"Well, at least we have water," said Old Hannah as she scooped a cup of water and slowly sipped. "In all my years I've never seen this well run dry."

"But we will miss our bread," said another.

Rachel filled her jar and hurried back home. "What will we do when we have no bread, Mama?" she asked as she poured the water into the large receptacle by the door.

"Don't worry, Rachel, God will take care of us," promised Mama. "He always does."

"But will we have bread?" asked Rachel intently.

Mama laughed. "Oh, Rachel, how you love your bread. But don't worry, I'm sure we'll have bread enough."

Rachel smiled and went out to play. Mama was right—Rachel did love bread! If she had to choose only one thing to eat, it would be bread. Papa said it was only because Mama made the best bread in the entire region. And Rachel couldn't argue with that. She had tasted other bread, but none as delicious as Mama's. Still she felt certain that even bad bread would be better than no bread at all.

One day at the well Rachel noticed how slow Old Hannah had become. "Can I help you?" she offered.

Old Hannah nodded. "Oh, that would be nice."

So Rachel drew Old Hannah's water and then offered to carry it all the way to her house, which was no small thing since Old Hannah lived at the far end of town. When they reached the house, Rachel went in to set the water down, but once inside the house she couldn't help but notice how very poor Old Hannah must be.

"Do you get enough to eat?" asked Rachel, her concern for the old woman growing as she noticed the barren shelves and empty food containers.

Old Hannah waved her hand. "Oh, I am just an old woman. No sense wasting valuable food on me."

Rachel blinked. "But what do you eat?"

"Oh, this and that. But food is scarce these days." Old Hannah closed her eyes, then smacked her lips. "But what I really miss the most is bread. Good hearty bread."

Rachel nodded eagerly. "I love bread too. I think I would die without it."

Old Hannah chuckled lightly. "I know how you feel." She glanced at the water jug. "Thanks for your help. I wish I had something to give you—like a thick piece of bread."

"Oh, that's all right," said Rachel. "If you like, I will help you with your water each day."

Old Hannah smiled faintly. "Thank you, Rachel, but I don't expect it will be too many more days now."

Rachel pondered Old Hannah's words as she returned to the well to fetch her own family's water. Was Old Hannah suggesting that she might not be around much longer? Was it possible she was starving to death? Rachel knew the old woman had no relatives around, no one to help or check on her. Rachel quickly filled her bucket, then hurried home. With each step a plan to help Old Hannah became clearer in her mind. Every day from now on Old Hannah would find a big chunk of the finest bread in the region after Rachel carried her water home for her. She was so excited about the plan that she wanted to run, but she knew better than to risk wasting water like that. And finally she arrived home without spilling a drop.

"Is it really getting that bad, Simon?" Rachel heard Mama ask Papa in a quiet and serious tone. Rachel, not wanting to interrupt, set down the jug and waited.

"Yes. If we're careful, our grain might last until next harvest. But one small loaf of bread must last our family for two days, and sometimes even three."

"Oh," said Mama. "That means only one small piece of bread at each meal—and that is practically nothing."

"I know. But it's the only way. Everyone, including our little bread lover, must understand—this is how we'll make it to the next harvest. And at least we have other foods to eat. Not as abundantly as usual, but we won't starve either."

"Yes," said Mama. "God will provide."

Rachel walked in and emptied the water, then began to help Mama with supper. As Rachel sliced a cucumber, Mama explained about the new plan for rationing bread. "I know this must disappoint you, Rachel."

Rachel nodded sadly. "Yes. You know how I love my bread." She continued slicing, still thinking of Old Hannah and how she loved bread too, but was starving. Then Rachel came up with a new idea. "Mama," she began carefully, not wanting to give it away, "you said we can have one small slice at each meal, right?"

"Yes, that's right."

"Well, you know how much I love a nice thick chunk of bread, don't you?"

"I know, and I'm sorry."

"No, that's not what I mean. Instead of having one thin slice at every meal, could I just have one nice fat slice for my midday meal?"

Mama smiled. "That would be fine, Rachel."

"Good."

The following day Rachel had no bread for breakfast. But at lunchtime Mama cut her a nice thick slice that Rachel pretended to nibble on and was tempted to just gobble up, but then she remembered Old Hannah, and when no one was looking she wrapped the precious bread in a cloth and tucked it in her skirt. Then later, just as planned, she carried Old Hannah's water, and when the old woman wasn't looking, without saying a word, Rachel left the wrapped piece of bread on the table, then quietly hurried away.

Day after day Rachel continued this practice. At first it was so difficult to see that thick slice of bread on her plate, yet not eat a single crumb. But after just one week her temptation lessened. And before long she noticed that Old Hannah was becoming stronger and stronger. Rachel began spending more time at Old Hannah's house and happily discovered the woman was a very gifted storyteller.

By the time the next harvest came (with more grain than ever), Old Hannah and Rachel were the best of friends. And soon Old Hannah was baking her own bread, which she shared generously with Rachel. One day as they sat eating a piece of freshly baked bread, Old Hannah told her a true story of One who called Himself the Bread of Life and gave all He had to save His friends. "I want to hear more about this man," said Rachel with real interest.

"You will, my dear," said Old Hannah. "You will." ✑

THE BREAD OF LIFE

As you walk down the aisles of a grocery store and see the wide variety of food that's available today, it's hard to believe that anyone would love bread more than anything like Rachel did. And when you look at how much food there is in a grocery store, it's almost harder to believe that anyone would need bread as much as Old Hannah did.

But not so long ago—and even for some today—bread was the most important daily food of all. Without bread many would have absolutely nothing to eat. It was like that when Jesus made His home on earth. At that time to be without bread most likely meant death by starvation. For bread was the most basic of basics—the sustenance of life.

So for Jesus to call Himself "the bread of life" was like saying, "You cannot live without Me." What a claim! And on top of that He said He was the bread that came from heaven and that no one could have eternal life unless they ate the bread that was His flesh. What did it all mean? Most didn't understand that He meant that one day He would give his life on the cross for their sins. And it is only by faith in what He accomplished on the cross that anyone can have eternal life. If you are trusting in Jesus for salvation, then you know exactly what it means for Him to be the Bread of Life.

"I am the bread of life. . . . I am the living bread

that came down out of heaven; if anyone eats of this bread,

he will live forever; and the bread also which I will

give for the life of the world is My flesh."

JOHN 6:48, 51 (NASB)

OUR PRAYER

Dear Jesus, thank You for being our Bread of Life—and for how You were willing to lay down Your life for us. We partake of Your life, though we don't understand everything about it. But we do it because we believe You, we trust You, and we love You. Amen.

Who is this man, nailed to the cross?

What has He done to warrant this loss?

Is He a criminal? What is His guilt?

Why is He dying, His blood being spilt?

Doesn't God notice His Son hanging there?

How can this be? Does anyone care?

He looks down upon them with love in His eyes.

The crucified hangs there and quietly dies.

THE SAVIOR

Being found in appearance as a man,
He humbled Himself by becoming obedient to the
point of death, even death on a cross.

PHILIPPIANS 2:8 (NASB)

One for All

❧ ⋮ ☙

Long ago there was a beautiful kingdom. On top of a hill, all the people lived within an enormous walled city. And right in the center there was a lovely and gracious palace, where the royal family lived.

Now the purpose of the huge wall around the city was to protect the people who lived inside from anyone who would want to invade and attack them. And this amazing wall was taller than ten men and wider than six oxen and made entirely of stone. For hundreds of years this incredible wall had protected everyone within the kingdom, keeping them safe from enemy invasions. The only way to get in or out was through a large drawbridge door that let down over a moat surrounding the wall, keeping everyone just as safe as can be.

Over the years the people of the kingdom had built more and more wooden houses and shops and buildings until the kingdom became quite a bustling, busy place. But there was room for all, and all were very happy within the safety of the kingdom walls.

The people in the kingdom loved both their king and their queen dearly. And they served them diligently and with a fierce loyalty. But even more than their king and queen, they loved their young son, the crown prince. Since the joyous day he had been born, the people had been devoted to the lad. And as he grew older, their love for him only grew stronger. For Prince Stephen was an exceptional boy. He was kindhearted and generous and brave. And he was always ready and willing to offer a helping hand or share a cheerful song. So much so that no one in the entire kingdom could ever find fault with their next king.

And so life continued happily and blissfully for everyone in this wonderful kingdom. Until one dark and bleak winter's day when someone inside one of the homes or shops allowed a small cooking fire to get out of hand, and before long several of the wooden buildings ignited.

Try as the people might, they just couldn't get the fire under control. Although no one had yet been injured, the fire was spreading fast!

"We must evacuate our kingdom before anyone is hurt," the king instructed the frightened crowd who had gathered in the square. "Now, don't worry about the loss of the buildings and such," he reassured them. "We can rebuild our homes and shops. But we cannot replace lives." Then he turned to his guards and gave the order only the king could give. "Lower the drawbridge immediately!"

The guards began to lower the door that was also the bridge, but it only opened for about a foot's width and then became stuck and wouldn't budge another inch. Try as they might, they couldn't move it.

By now the people were becoming frantic, for the smoke and flames were getting closer with each moment, and what had once been their haven of safety would soon become a death trap.

"Let us out!" cried a woman, clutching her baby.

"Help us!" cried a little girl as she looked at the flames quickly approaching.

Suddenly Prince Stephen, who was also an excellent climber, began to scale the partially opened door.

"What are you doing, son?" cried out the queen.

"I think I can fit through that small space," cried Prince Stephen. "I'll see what's keeping the bridge closed. Maybe I can fix it somehow."

"Hurrah!" cried the people. "Prince Stephen will save us. Prince Stephen has come to the rescue!"

He heard their cheers and shouts of encouragement as he reached the top of the bulky door. But he also saw the flames coming quickly closer as he slipped through the small opening, just barely, then eased himself down to where he could see the problem. A large piece of timber had become stuck, and try as he might from his precarious position, he couldn't put enough force on the stubborn and heavy board to even budge it. Yet from within the walls he could hear the screams and cries as the flames steadily approached.

"I see you, son!" called the king from the top of the wall. "It looks like you've found the problem. Can you fix it?"

"I hope so," yelled Prince Stephen. He thought that perhaps if he wrapped himself around the board and pulled with all of his strength, it just might move. "I'm going to give it one big try now, Father."

"Be careful, son!"

Prince Stephen wrapped his arms and legs around the board and pulled with all his might, and amazingly the board sprang free. But now the prince was dangling precariously over the edge of the wall high in the air with no way down but to fall many stories to certain death. And the screams of his people, trapped inside, were louder than ever.

"Lower it now!" he yelled to his father.

The king paused just for a brief moment, his heart breaking in two as he made his decision, the only decision he could possibly make. He looked back over the wall to where his people were about to perish in the flames.

"Lower the door!" the king commanded loudly, his voice carrying above all the sounds of crackling fire and yelling people. And in that same instant, with a loud, heavy boom, the enormous door went down.

The people quickly poured out of the burning kingdom in a thick stream, running eagerly over the lowered drawbridge and happily out into the green hillside of sweet freedom. They shouted and rejoiced that the door had finally opened, just in the nick of time, and that every single one of them had all made it out safely and alive!

All but one.

For you see, Prince Stephen died that day. He understood there was no other way to open that door than for him to lay down his life. So he willingly gave his own life so he could preserve the lives of all his dearly loved friends and family. He could have done nothing less, and he could have given no more. ❧

THE SAVIOR

As you think about the story of Prince Stephen, it is easy to find similarities between what he did and what Jesus did on the cross. Both were gentle and kind and dearly loved their people. Both hung from a piece of wood and gave their lives willingly so others could live. Both of their deaths were witnessed by their fathers.

But that is where the comparison ends. You see, there is more, much more to the sacrifice made by Christ on the cross. He was not just a boy who would someday be king. He was the Prince of Peace, the King of kings, the God of heaven and earth. Yes, He had taken on human form, but the one who gave His life for us was also the perfect Lamb of God.

And the people Christ died for were not loyal, loving servants like those who followed Prince Stephen. Jesus went to the cross and gave His life for those who despised Him. Those who mocked and scorned Him. Those who were His enemies. And most amazing of all, He did it willingly!

The biggest difference, though, comes at the end of the story. For Prince Stephen death was his final act, but not for Jesus. Three days after suffering on the cross He rose from the grave. Death could not hold Him. And because of all He did, we can have eternal life. His story ends with rejoicing—with life—because He reigns with His Father, and someday we will reign with Him.

He Himself bore our sins in His body on the cross,

so that we might die to sin and live to righteousness;

for by His wounds you were healed.

1 PETER 2:24 (NASB)

OUR PRAYER

Dear Jesus, how can we begin to thank You for the way You gave Your life on the cross? How can we show our gratitude for the way You took our sin upon Yourself, surrendering Your relationship with Your own Father? You did this amazing thing just so we could have eternal life with You. The only way we can really thank You is to give our lives to You. Amen.

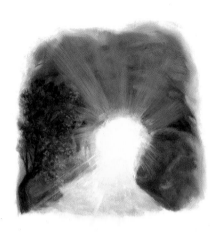

Who is this man? Where has He gone?

The tomb is empty and He lives on!

The grave couldn't hold Him. He's had victory!

He's conquered death for you and for me!

Who is this man? What does He give?

He gives us His life so that we may live.

Glorious heaven now waits for us.

He's opened the gates—His name is Jesus.

AN INVITATION FOR YOU

❧ ⋅ ❧

As you have gone through this book, you have heard some of the wonderful names of Jesus! And His names show us how much He loves us. Perhaps you already know Him as a personal friend, or maybe you have never asked Him to come into your life to be your Savior. If you haven't but you want to now, you can pray something like this:

> *"Dear Jesus, I am really sorry for the bad things that I have done. Thank You for dying for me so that I can live forever with You in heaven someday. I want You to come and live in my heart. I want You to be my Savior and my very best friend."*

If you would like to know more about Jesus or would like to tell us that you have prayed in this way to Jesus, please write us. And if you would like some more literature about Jesus, we would love to send it to you.

Good News Publishers/Crossway Books
1300 Crescent Street
Wheaton, Illinois 60187

Creating Christ-Centered Traditions

⌘ ⋅ ⌘

O Come Let Us Adore Him can be enjoyed on its own, but is also a perfect companion to FamilyLife's popular family Christmas resource, Adorenaments, found in tens of thousands of homes across the country. The twelve names of Christ in *O Come Let Us Adore Him* correspond to the twelve names represented in FamilyLife's Adorenaments. So you can use all or parts of each chapter along with your Adorenaments as a fun, interactive way to experience Jesus and learn more about Him.

Along with this book, a series of products have been designed to complement FamilyLife's Adorenaments with the goal of equipping families to understand that Jesus is more than just a baby in a manger and to help children and adults gain a broader perspective of who He really is.

Special, Christ-centered traditions at Christmas draw families together and create lasting memories. But traditions don't just happen—they require prayerful preparation. By using the complementary resources below—any of which can be easily adapted for use in Sunday school, children's programs, or special gatherings with friends and neighbors—you can develop fun and meaningful traditions for this Christmas and for many years to come.

The Christ-centered materials built around Adorenaments include:

ADORENAMENTS
FamilyLife, a division of Campus Crusade for Christ, Inc.

A completely redesigned set of twelve colorful ornaments, each representing a biblical name of Christ, comes with a family devotional booklet. Available in the fall of 2001.

O COME LET US ADORE HIM
Crossway Books

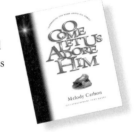

A beautifully illustrated family gift book with original poems, stories, and reflections all focused on twelve names of Christ.

ADORE HIM MUSIC CD/CASSETTE
Frank and Betsy Hernandez; distributed by Straightway

These twelve lively Scripture-memory songs correspond to Adorenaments. In addition, Adore Him includes special narrations by Steve Green, Rebecca St. James, Kay Arthur, John MacArthur, and others.

WHAT NICK & HOLLY FOUND IN GRANDPA'S ATTIC
ZonderKidz

The story of two children who learn the true meaning of Christmas as they discover twelve treasures from the past, which Grandpa uses to explain the different names of Jesus.

ADORENAMENTS ACTIVITY BOOK
FamilyLife, a division of Campus Crusade for Christ, Inc.

This creative, reproducible companion to Adorenaments is especially for Sunday school or classroom teachers.

Help the children you love:

* ✳ construct and color their own set of Adorenaments.
* ✳ prepare a special booklet that recalls and explains the names of Jesus Christ.
* ✳ creatively interact with the biblical names of Jesus through fun crafts.

THIS BOOKLET IS BEING REDESIGNED WITH ADORENAMENTS FOR RELEASE IN FALL 2001.

For more information
on any of these delightful resources,
visit your local Christian bookstore
or contact FamilyLife at 1-800-FL-TODAY
or visit us at www.familylife.com.